THE DIRT RIDDLES

The Dirt Riddles

POEMS BY

MICHAEL WALSH

The University of Arkansas Press

Fayetteville

2010

ISBN-10: 1-55728-925-5
ISBN-13: 978-1-55728-925-4

14   13   12   11   10   5   4   3   2   1

Designed by Liz Lester

⊗ The paper used in this publication meets the minimum requirements
of the American National Standard for Permanence of Paper
for Printed Library Materials Z39.48-1984.

LIBRARY OF CONGRESS CATALOGING-IN-PUBLICATION DATA

Walsh, Michael, 1973-
The dirt riddles : poems / by Michael Walsh.
    p.   cm.
ISBN-13: 978-1-55728-925-4 (pbk. : alk. paper)
ISBN-10: 1-55728-925-5
I. Title.
PS3623.A4465D57   2010
811'.6—dc22
2009046590

ACKNOWLEDGMENTS

These poems have appeared, sometimes in different forms, in the following journals.

Alaska Quarterly Review: "Against Pastorals"
Birmingham Poetry Review: "Haying the Fields"
Blue Mesa Review: "Milkweed"
Chattahoochee Review: "Quilt Rags," "Weekly Horoscope"
DIAGRAM: "Grounding," "Landscape with Forgotten Machines"
The Fourth River: "Inheritance," "Shore"
Great River Review: "After His Lessons from the Belt," "Plantings,"
    "A Table Prayer"
Meridian: "On Kissing My Husband at a Gas Station," "Three
    Self-Portraits in a Dress"
Inch: "Names for Ditch Flowers"
The Midwest Quarterly: "Star Chart," "Wind"
The New York Quarterly: "Pinup" (as "Pinup Girl")
The North American Review: "Tornado Junk"
Permafrost: "Buffalo Bones," "Mud, Apples, Milk"
Southern Poetry Review: "The Flood"

"After His Lessons from the Belt," "Haying the Fields," "I Leave the House for the Storm," "New Tenants," "Plantings," and "A Table Prayer" appeared in my chapbook *Adam Walking the Garden,* published by Red Dragonfly Press.

I'd like to thank the following writers who saw versions of these poems, encouraged my vision, and helped me from the start so long ago to the finish: Robert Hedin, Robin Metz, Rachel Moritz, Josie Rawson, and Sheryl St. Germain.

Likewise, I couldn't have completed this manuscript without the years of kindness and support from the faculty in the English Department at the University of Minnesota. Thanks for keeping me around.

For Adam Nelsen

CONTENTS

I.

II.

III.

IV.

I.

MORNING MILKINGS

Mother slaps every sleeping cow
with a chapped, leathery hand.
Once, twice, as many times as it takes.
Then, with the lightest touch, she announces
to the first startled flank
her bucket, her brown paper towels, her iodine,
her plastic syringes for the sick.
She washes each udder,
overripe and leaking
faster into the rag
with each wipe, careful
of any touchy warts.
One long squeeze
into her palm and she's done.
The milk's ripe and opaque
in her lifeline,
no flecks of red
today, no odd clots.
A skeptic, she pushes
her greasy glasses
back up her nose, closer
to her nearsighted eyes,
then tosses the sample, quick as spit.

Wind

If you sprint fast enough,
the corn runs with you,
whole rows quick on their roots.

Slow down and they jog
calm and breathless.
Stop and they turn

to walls. Hands on knees,
you pant, and all the leaves,
like wings, beat wildly.

HAYING THE FIELDS

My father high on the John Deere,
the baler chewing row after row
of cut alfalfa, mustard, thistle.
I can't tell, as I lift and stack,
how many small lives
die here, mangled under twine.

In the loft we stack the load,
fresh green dust
a snowfall, bundles wrapped
tight as butcher's meat.

Later I throw one down the chute
and knife its twine. A snake
bursts from the folds,
its last thrash rigored.

Smell what the bale exhales:
not sweet, green field: mold.
I feed the herd this bread.

FLYOVER

These flatlands float murky as negatives.
So much hasn't been exposed: sun

cindering each night in alkali dirt,
darknesses asleep inside white cows.

No one notices where stones, huge as houses,
bust topsoil, bald rock ledges.

In their keyless, windowless rooms
fossil fish still swim in mineral.

Above, ditch blooms swarm the open road.
Frogs hop the gravel where a car drove by,

their eyes wide and itching in the dust.

NAMES FOR DITCH FLOWERS

Here's the smoking bloom, embers lighting its root.
Here's the viper hatching from an aster's stem.
Here's the roost for many flightless orange birds.

Here's another waving its horns at my palm.
And here, a crop of ripening bells,
a hydra of needles.

First Kisses

Out of sight, I kissed brown, crumbly pasture,
gray coral of antlers, daddy longlegs
cupped quivering, but not my mother, father,
or any boy. I kissed light condensed

in milky quartz, limestone pregnant with shells,
puddles where drowned earthworms
settled, soft roots and rotting sticks, but not my face
puckered in the car's scalding mirror.

I kissed white cats who slept underneath
cows, rusted rain barrels where June bugs
scrabbled in water, and fresh mud,
telltale impressions I wanted you to find.

SHORE

The deeper I walk into the field,
the higher, the wetter
the bluestem, the more leaves
flash their weed-tangled silver.
Hidden everywhere,
swaying, thistle and nettles
bristle, all spine and stinger.
From ankle to thigh
they scratch their names
for tadpoles that turn
to beetles, eels to roots,
and fish to mice.
Now touch this slash, that sting.
The mouth can't speak them,
but the skin, that strange tongue,
starts to mutter.

PLANTINGS

Weed snubs, snapped taproots,
sheared rocks: *an alphabet*
the last harvest shattered.
All day I pitch stones.
On the hay rack they vibrate
like kernels, ready to sprout
root or word.
                    Thistle, pigweed,
ditch rose. The first words
take root in flight,
in rippling passages. All day
I wander leaf shadows, tip
my hat to polite rot.

BUFFALO BONES

My father sprang the first bone
loose from the sod by luck.
He gripped the rib. Felt it
anchor. He touched the chest,
the rough fur. And dug
for days until he tore the beast
free, the vertebrae
packed tight, broken.

He carried the skeleton
into the scrub brush for keeping.
We rode on its back
under the leaves, listened
to the herd travel underground—
that clatter and thump of hooves.
We called them like cows.
We were sure they could hear our bare feet
stomp the dark clouds of dirt.

AFTER HIS LESSONS FROM THE BELT

my mother would always sit on the bed
and spread out the great map
of his fault lines—that webwork
of unpredictable tensions.
We studied where the quakes
were most likely to occur: in barns, fields
near sheds.

       We learned to sense the shifting,
the slow grind of plates, the opening
chasms of his hands.

SOLO

Outside the shed, our ears would go queasy
from that caterwaul of dull blade

against grinding stone,
the axe handle an instrument

tuned to our father's grip.
Steel lids echoed like empty seats.

Fingers crammed, we listened
to blood thump and vibrate

in the quiet of the inner ear, the din
he sparked from the shining smear

where his face reflected in steel.
The metal whimpered and blared

whenever he made the air
break into blue dust and fire.

BULLY

I turn myself into a rock.
Tim grabs me from the floor.
We go to break what litters

his backyard: glass bottles,
dismembered doll parts,
plastic soldiers in a skirmish.

His brother's toys.
We bust the buildings.
We roll through trenches

on both sides. It's love.
I'm helpless and strong
when he squeezes.

He lifts me to his brother's face,
those sweet and full lips.
I love Tim's fist.

ROCK PICKING

In the bed of the truck: whole gourds
the earth couldn't crack,

eggs that never hatch or rot.
They quaver, roll, and collide.

Under the rock pile's seal of moss
limestone and chalk get crushed,

white bits and wet
powder flecked with fossils.

Warm in your palm, one chunk
bears the paw print of the old forest.

When light creeps through
the dark heat of your squeeze,

the leaf bends and breathes.
Like doorless huts

shells protrude from slabs. All shut-ins.
Only rain draws their antennae

through the roofs, listening
for branches breaking underfoot.

GROUNDING I

Ticking louder
against the electric fence,

weak in the crossed mess of stems,
weeds break under your stick.

An underground signal
beats unbreakable in the roots.

Brush a leaf, a wire by accident,
and you turn the wrong dial.

The sudden, terrible sun
pounds the air white,

the ground black as static.
For hours after

your fingertips babble, their prints
strange as radio waves.

II.

AGAINST PASTORALS

I'd lay my hand on her warm hide
and inside her a calf
thrashed like a carp. And a hoof
would kick my palm, a splash
no one else could hear.
I'd leave to feed the newborns,
able to turn but just barely,
plastic tags popped through their ears
and black scabs in between
where I burned off their horns,
white nubs soft as roots.
That scorched fur stank like human hair.
I turned and knew what I had to celebrate.
Outside I saw our pastures,
fences, the gates that connected it all,
and the stock pond, brackish water
where the cows would stand
for hours swatting flies, a kind of time
their tails kept, no different than the piece
of straw in my mouth, a dirty reed
I sucked and blew, tuneless.

FOOD CHAIN

after a line from Roethke

Nothing would keep in that kitchen.
The walls sweated mold, and flies
hatched from cracks like spores

even in November, when frost bloomed
on the stuck window. In a day
bananas went black,

their peels slick as dead fish.
Milk turned chemical overnight.
Each morning I held my breath,

tossed whatever was foul
into that bucket: bad fruit and milk,
green yolks, membranes

of lettuce. In the house
it was refuse, but in the barnyard
it was champagne I could pour

over the crowded snouts,
the splash of amber foam
their daily basting.

A Table Prayer

Buckets of manure—the rheumy broth
God made the world from—
what we spread on gardens, tree rows
so the leaves and fruit ripen.
O, blessed manure, we gather
your new flesh—sweet corn
and greens—we set our table.

WEEKLY HOROSCOPE

Grandma spread the local paper
across her vinyl tablecloth
the way a psychic would prepare
her worn stack of cards.

Then she flipped to the obituaries,
passed the magnifying glass
back and forth over the black facts
in search of that wonderful day

when she'd read her name, and know.

OVERDUE

Amounts due massing like flies
to his name, my father said,
I must smell like meat. Sunburned
arm stretched across the table,

he asked God to chop. His fist
hit Formica like the butcher's blow.
My startled arm swooped beneath.
Don't worry, he said. *The numbers,*

they're morphine. They fill you silly
before you're ever born: blood tests,
due dates, birth weights. Don't worry,
kid, they won't collect for years.

But I understood *systole, diastole,*
checked my wrist for the sound
of numbers louder than my name,
darker than the dollar's ink.

BARN CLOTHES

Same size, my parents stained and tore
alike in the barn, their brown hair

ripe as cow after twelve hours of gutters.
At supper they spoke in jokey moos.

Sure, showers could dampen that reek
down to a whiff under fingernails, behind ears,

but no wash could wring the animal from their clothes:
one pair, two pair, husband, wife, reversible.

ANIMAL DIARY

Shepherd

An hour ago I took
their new calf on a rope,
and now they stand at the gate,
a thumbless mob at a door.
The mother's bellor
goes off like a shot.
Her wild eye has found me
here, near the fence.
She lifts her muzzle
above the wires,
her nostrils dark
as gun barrels.

Barn Cat

The daredevil, he's asleep
in the straw under his favorite cow,
her massive, damp belly
the pillow that kills.
I snatch his tail
and swing him, fangs startled, swiping the air.
One day she'll squash him
flat and bloodless
as the rest, and I'll lift
all his broken parts, mouth
his last hiss and shake him,
like this, over the gutter.

June Calf

Breath to bone
I hear him scramble

for a foothold.
You tie a rope

like a tow chain and tug
and tug until he skids loose,

smacks his shadow
headfirst.

Matriarch

Today the vet drugged
the last girl with horns,
the bossy goddess
of a hornless herd.
Thirteen years old,
they were hard and dark as oak.
I watched him whittle
her points to slivers,
then pare the bone
close to the core and saw
and saw her regal head
down to a stump, small
and weak as her sisters'.

Fly Grammar

The blowflies begin
in the sweet meats
of small-boned bodies.

In the cages of plagues
God handfeeds
they nip at His hand.

Loose barnside,
they land on the yellow
glue strip, twisting,

mouthless tongue
they kiss and become,
black vowels whining.

SURROGATES

Mother would push her hand inside the cow
slow, up to the elbow,
make the animal arch its back

to the right curve
for her silver gun,
steady and quick as a stud.

Months later her child slid
loose from the womb. I stood
with my mother, watched

the cow push and push that perfect head
past the sopping braid of a gutter tail,
and oh, how his eyes

would roll open, a stare
both sad and amazed.
In the sink I mixed that first milk:

tap water and his ration
of sticky, sour powder.
My hand tight on the nipple,

he pulled and pressed so hard
the bottle dug into my ribs,
even popped open and spilled.

As a special treat, I offered
my fingers, their skin wrinkled
and tasteless, but like a teat.

Mooo

Now here's sorrow
pushed young from ribs.
One part bassoon
two parts howl,
it vibrates, inner

ear to marrow
and larynx, comes
to rest in solar plexus
long enough for you
to bellor likewise.

New Tenants

This April autumn comes early.
Wild roses bloom in ditches.
They auction our cattle, tractors, even our plows.
For weeks corn bones stand in the fields.
Then the weeds charge the old wheel ruts.
In May they'll build their million sails
from the leaf-rot, launch each crew
with the order to occupy.

FAMILY FARM

Let the garden eat its own green vines.
Let the yard riot back to ditch
and the field brood seedy with weeds.

Someone should live there, they say.
Not me, he says. *Not me,* she says.
Not us, they agree. *You, you.*

Whoever you are, no one knows
how many violets sway
underfoot out here, how much thistle.

MUD, APPLES, MILK

Of all things to miss, it's silly
to miss how cows drowse in mud.
They blink slow as toads.
Instead I should miss
light on the blond corn
or trails of gravel dust
that rose like kites and vanished.

But I don't miss that.
I miss how I could bring
bruised apples, press them
like smelling salts
to sleepy noses.
You had to let go
real fast or risk a finger
to the lick and snap.

I miss their udders too,
the mud fresh as wax
on the swollen skin.
Each day I broke the seals
with hot rags, and milk
flooded my palm—
a white creek down
the gulley of my wrist.

EVENING MILKINGS

Even now when I stand at the gate
and call their names, they come,
trusting as the animals that went on the ark.
To make my penance
I give them back their neck chains,
their swarming hides of flies.
I spray their bitten flanks,
then lock them down
for my father to milk.
And to one bold cow,
the one who will kick him tonight,
I give my name,
my hands, my face and legs,
my whole body.
I watch her thumbs
work the cold lock from her neck.
Then I stand frightened
in her stall and kick that man
when he raises the pitchfork.
Like a good beast
I jerk hard on the chain.

III.

STALK, ROOT, SCISSORS

Milkweed

Grandma and I cut milkweed
in the ditch. She slashes. I'm good

for gathering the stalks, the pods
packed and damp with feathers.

The ends ooze watery white.
I choke the tips until they run dry,

the stuff all over my jeans,
make them drip so much

my fingers stick. *Don't touch
your lips,* she says. *That milk*

will make you go blind.
But I love to crush this cataract sap

from the stems, lift it
runny from the wrist, and lick.

I Leave the House for the Storm

Pines pitch the yard.
Flashes break heaven
black as field dirt.
You are too tall,
I remember Grandma saying
when I climbed high
on the thick rafters of the oak,
Lightning will get you.
For miles the clouds tighten—
ready to collapse their cliff
of water. I watch the current
pull and pull like stitches
until a branch splinters
the sky, sights its pole or tree,
its trunk of human body.

Quilt Rags

Every time we molt our blue jeans,
Grandma takes the busted pairs.
First she trims that feathery fringe
from the worn-out knees.

Then she hangs them
over a cardboard box, unravels
long, golden threads from the seams,
and razors the empty legs

down to spare parts, squares
and triangles for her quick pins.
The awkward crotch she cuts last,
pulls out the zipper like a gizzard.

BLANKET GAME

Sundays I'd creep onto the blanket and wait
in the warm wedge between my father's knees.
I didn't know when, but they'd snap shut,
gotcha, and I wriggled
helpless in that cotton placenta, dark and humid
between his thighs, my breath gone
with the first squeeze—funny, then longer and too long
and impossible. My lips mouthed swear words,
my palms pried at his kneecaps,
and all he did was grunt, then clamp tighter,
his leg muscles so strong
I went slack in their playful hold
and spilled loose, panting, when he let me.

BURLESQUE

In my father's throat
the songs would get stuck
for days, burbling loose,
swallowed quiet,
and then in the shower
he screeched, his voice
a teenage crooner's.
It's his virgin wail,
my mother joked.
Get your ear plugs.
Behind the plastic curtain
of his stage, he yodelled
and woofed; he purred,
warbled, and trilled.
For the finale he strutted
through the house, one towel
around his waist, another
positioned like a wig
on his cropped hair.
His belly jiggled
like a well-fed diva's.
When he raised his hand
and bellowed that last
wordless, mocking note,
he let the towel slip from his hips.

CAMOUFLAGE

I sneak through the hot cloud,
my glasses left behind

like a crutch. The other boys
soap themselves in the spray

until the light inside
their skin is shining.

Steam blurs them strange
as X-rays of angels,

but they dim and gray
into the shower haze. I stop

and fade too. Then someone
bumps my hidden body.

One touch and we startle
scarlet, hair frightened

ankle to ear.

PINUP

I'd help my best friend
unfold the center girl,
that cowboy hat
in her hand, his stare
demanding and blank.
From her pages
I learned how to pose
down on my knees,
take off my clothes
piece by piece, purse my lips
and pout, her red
press-on nails
suddenly sharp
on my fingers.
Even my skinny
chest would wobble
fake with breasts
until I got comfortable
on the page, male again,
and watched his shaking
hand undo each
cold, steel button.

THE DIRT RIDDLES

Tell me, what are the women and men?
Weeds without roots to bind them.

The houses? Helmets for the horizon.

And the plows? Teeth of the marching armies
who drag their appetites like sacks,

the field a bed where the living
and dead bump bones in passing.

The cow? Heart of a greater creature.

What happened to her years of milk?
Femurs for dogs to gnaw,
pitchforks dressing in flies again.

The graves? All coffins into bonnets.

The flowers and grass going wild, thistle
rising where people walk?

Mold to leaven the children's bread.

FIELD JUNK

Instead of scrap, I'm harvesting bolts
unscrewed from Frankensteins,
springs sizzling with rust.

Cord, hinge, tube, and bone:
repurposed, I pick them,
assemble the diagram of a man

on my dirt drawing board, bust him
back to junk, rebuild. Spare parts,
I lay experimental in his place.

EAR, SKIN, AND BONE RIDDLES

From the field's flatline
center, the horizon of dirt

extends underground
toward the rumbles

your ear can't hear,
migrating noises

strong as hurricanes
but meek on the surface

where, walking
lines of tilled earth

like crude latitudes,
you likewise hum.

꩜

Pitching rocks against stones,
you start to feel faceless

as the heap, wordless
except for the clack

and clatter. They roll
to a stop, balance

monklike, and settle,
sometimes atop each other,

on their mats of moss.

꩜

In storm light, everything's hinge:
your wet shoulders, the lilac's petals,

tree line, the clouds, that blue peek
to elsewhere. You step into the open.

Rain's knocking out the blooms in mouthfuls.
Rain, like a runner on the matted leaves.

Water trickles down your glasses,
onto lips, finds your tongue next,

and tricks your throat to swallow.
Now the storm wanders your blood.

꩜

The crabapple poised between rot
and sweetness knows it has no choice—

eaten either way.
Bugs name any cavity *Mother.*

᷎

To leave your body, you have to trick
your bones, right hand first.

Left hand, look the other way.
Forget the thumb and grow feathers.

Feet, petrify. Heart, molder.
Mind, seep homeless into runoff.

Don't come back in skin,
come back in chitin

or scales, with the bright
frond of brain uncoiling.

GROUNDING II

Once, he let me touch that fresh ink,
barbed wire around his arm.

I felt the strands turn electric
where they crossed veins,

drew his pulse to the surface.
Beneath my inept fingers

throbbed that line, strong
as a meridian. It circled

down through blood, to muscles
pinned bone by bone,

to iridescence spinning,
holding still. The stars,

far from his skin.
They thudded and hummed.

Then my dumb fingers
fumbled the ebb and flow.

STAR CHART

The fireflies ignite like matches.
All around they drift
and fade, their trails erratic
as comets. Each night
they move their migrant galaxy
in the grass, one spindrift
star after another. Where they pause,
they form a cave mouth
leading gradually underground
to rocks that orbit the core.

Lovers at Night with a Quilt

Legs snapping coneflowers,
we shamble past the hill
where mice roam
through a deer's rib cage
pierced by grass.
Stars behind clouds
and this blanket
we lay down
won't light us.

I've lost my hand
in your shadow,
grope your cheek
to find fingers.
Kiss me, hard and dark.
Take root in my mouth
even when mosquitoes tap
the hum of my veins.

FIELD BURNING

With milk of motor oil
we feed our weed-and-stick nest.
One match and seed burns
the wind, catches on
shirt cuffs, hatching.

Brushing them off all morning
we dig line to corral the char.
Hair fries. Blisters swell
germlike, full of sea
beneath fingerprints.

The black about to gust,
flames grab for the green.
At the edge, sprouting
stubble and scrappy blooms
howl gray at our boots.

IV.

INHERITANCE

Rust blooms across my land:
spots like mold on white cars,
their spark plugs cold as insects
poisoned in orange powder.
It's already been to the house,

screwed the preserves
shut for good. In the shed
I touch the many red, ripe
nail points. They pollinate
the pale flowers of my hands.

THE FLOOD

Tonight the river rises
in the chest of drawers.
Boxes drift from shelves,
and the whole house leaks
from every socket.

Room by room,
it's going down,
the floor buckling.
In the kitchen, flowers
from the tablecloth
climb onto
the wallpaper
up to the ceiling.

And when it wells
under my tongue,
when it runs down
my throat and spills
from my lips,
I say, *River,*
Let me breathe you.

PAPER FLESH

Each year I page through my young father's comics,
more jaundiced now, more dry moth
but still smelling of smoke from the night
the mice chewed the fire to life
inside those rented walls. I remember
the insulation burning hidden, the hour
he had to ransack our past, crammed
unexamined in every closet and drawer.
Maskless in the smoke,
he dropped flimsy cardboard boxes
out windows, tossed clothes
with hangers still inside,
the shape of malformed wings.
For a moment I was awake
in the car, confused.
Then men ran everywhere
on the lawn, one hose
aimed at the blaze,
the dresser open on its side
with a white gush of cotton.
But the water failed to appear or vanished.
Somehow, against all common sense,
my father walked into the house.
He couldn't leave these stacks behind.
But the bright covers were already half-cooked,

dark as negatives, heroes and villains
singed indistinguishable.
He never read them again. I do
not for the stories so much as the scorch marks,
the faint pictures of that boy.

NEWSPAPERS FROM 1929

The fume from the baseboard,
dry and stifling as mummy, gets me.
Ear pressed to the white wall, eyes shut,

brain wide open,
I listen to the packed mash of pages
ferment yellow inside the walls.

In windstorms the roof,
rickety binding, creaks open.
I wait. Depression dust spills

inside the crevice
shaped like an hourglass.
Plaster and paper bits

fall too. The house shifts.
Names of window jumpers hang
suspended, some bulging

between rafters. I rip
handfuls of gibberish,
puzzle pieces confounding as sky.

DRAGLINE

To hang easy
in the black heat of the eaves

like the spiders
is what I want, to forget

up and *down*, learn *ground*
no matter direction.

It won't be web from my wrist.
It's root, not thread,

they use to dangle
happily handless,

float like pollen,
attach anew.

Three Self-Portraits in a Dress

I'm tugging the fussy, nylon zipper
all the way up my back
until my mother's dress
fits, ridiculous
hippie yellow with flowers.
In front of this mirror
I'm posing flat chested
with ape legs and no razor.
I'm a boy again, dragging
this hem into the yard
to play in the shell of a tire,
rainwater rocking
in its stale middle.
I'm my mother too,
still able to fit
into her favorite dress,
pot and rolling papers
in the hidden pocket
and soon the soup
of a baby boy
cooking in this belly.
Stuck, I wriggle
from the clammy fabric,
my elbow tearing
the frail stitches, the zipper
jammed halfway.

Handmade for Disasters

Grandma would fuss with quilt patterns,
obsess about alignment
like a mechanic,
the hidden needles
quick to bloody a finger.
She pinned and unpinned
the stale squares, eager
to perfect these gifts
shipped from her church.

I find an extra
years later in a drawer,
an American flag
shredded to mouse rags
on the first hard wash.
It lay on someone's bed
a week at most
but I remember the months
she ripped and cut
the mildewed Christmas sweaters,
blue jeans busted at the knees, bedsheets,
washed clean as used can be.

I wonder how many evaporated
to fog, wrapped tight and tearing
around people passed out
blissful from exhaustion, their beds
deep in river water or taken
through the missing roof
and flung to the next county.

Tornado Junk

Above the news breaking in the ticker,
we watch the funnels like a parade

over our lake: frogs like candies
tossed to amateur cameramen, boats

let go on helium winds. Now, live,
one's ripping its own road.

We hear buzz saw wings at work
in the real distance, right outside,

a fracas of glass and black noise.
Afterwards, we take stock of the landscape:

twenty-foot-long weeds wrapped
dripping around the elms,

this beer bottle green with algae,
set down capped, upright, drinkable,

which I point out twice before I see
where the scene has taken you:

our blue car, a net of gasping fish
lodged in the windshield. One eye

opens against the kaleidoscope of yours,
the bright tunnel slowly turning.

ON KISSING MY HUSBAND AT A GAS STATION

It's a dirty peck,
quick as a feather.
And now no one else in line
can bear to look at us.
Their gazes flutter from gum
on cheap racks to bottles
or keys they clutch, careful
until we step to the counter.
Then their eyes lock
hard and blank on our backs.
The warm, uncomfortable spot
shifts between my shoulder blades.
I turn and glare at two guys
long enough to break
their stare, fixed now
on their worn-out, Bible-black boots.
It's our bad luck
that they wheel onto the street
right behind us,
their high beams in our mirrors.
We can't see the road, just that awful light
accelerating in the lane behind us,
their searchlight fast and cold.

LANDSCAPE WITH FORGOTTEN MACHINES

Searching the creeping charlie and wild grape
you can't tell fallen branch from axle,

barbed wire from the vine that burns
like a fuse through the tangle.

Two box elders have twisted their trunks
through a plow's rusted frame, landlocked

the blades. On a hay rack's gray slats
a field of thick, dusty mold blooms.

Somewhere inside these thorns and burrs:
car batteries black and juicy with acid,

deflated innertubes that stick like leeches
to the dirt. And underneath the plants and junk,

rust welds together the lost washer rings.
Bolts hibernate like seeds. Screws burrow.

WISH

When I kiss him, weed sour
and tomato green
after hours in this garden,
I taste the darkness
suspended between bone and skin,
the loam and manure
we eat through bright leaves.
In his pebble-torn hands
I'm white butcher paper,
unwrapped outside for the feast.
My nipple ripens
fast in his mouth.
But first, in my hand,
the hose hiccups
its hot spray into the grass.
I'd like to be the jet of water
that breaks over his skin,
the lucky stream that touches
and tastes him all at once,
every finger a tongue.

GARDEN AND GRAVE

Annual

Each year I come back
to this ball of barbed wire.
Grass roots have wrapped
the strands like a double helix,
but I pull and rip the mass.

I try to unwind the tangles.
They bare their teeth,
sweet with disease.
They spring and bend
and knot again.

When I take off my gloves,
useless, I see my fingers,
how the cotton liner
clots these punctures,
swollen red from rust.

Junk Garden

Out of tin can beds, out of wheel rims,
out of stacks of axles

trunks bend, bark scars.
In the jumble of aphids and rust

serial numbers breed with beetles
and seeds, bond to topsoil, my skin.

Another minute and they hive.
Another hour and they empire.

Native

Thunder vibrates for miles.
In every field, ditch, and garden
the seeds burst and uncurl
like larval wings.

To the trees I offer my leg bone.
To the grass, my dead hair.
And to this dirt, all eighty acres of clay and leaf-rot,
I offer this flowerless, ripening flesh.

And now I sink into this field.
And from my last rib
one black flower
rises, not knowing its name,
whether it belongs or invades.

Garden and Grave

A femur digs itself up
and starts to shovel out ribs.

Deer, manured cats,
crows eaten and shat out

jerk themselves up
from their common grave.

At dawn the sunflowers lift
their heads, eager to chew the light.

Muttering, I Pour Gas into the Ditch

Forget this stabbed eye,
these stems bristling
with pig hair, this viper
climbing the air
with no ladder.

Ditch rose,
I light this trickle
with your spine.
Help me clear
the tangle for the dead.